Frost & Found: A Winter Mystery at the Ice Hotel

This cozy winter mystery book promises twists, turns, and surprises to keep you guessing until the final page.

Violet Frost Mysteries
Book 1

Evangeline Winters

Copyright © 2024 by Evangeline Winters

All rights reserved.

No part of this book may be reproduced in any form or by any electronic or mechanical means, including information storage and retrieval systems, without written permission from the author, except for the use of brief quotations in a book review.

Contents

Prologue: The Arrival	1
1. COLD COMFORT	7
2. ECCENTRIC SUSPECTS	13
3. THE FROZEN BODY	19
4. AN ICY LABYRINTH	26
5. COLD HEARTS	33
6. WARMING UP TO THE TRUTH	40
7. THE ICE BREAKS	46
8. FROST & FOUND	53
9. EPILOGUE: WARMTH IN UNEXPECTED PLACES	58
10. AFTERWORD: REFLECTIONS ON SYNESTHESIA	62
From the Desk of Violet Frost	62
11. A NOTE FROM THE AUTHOR	64

Prologue: The Arrival

Violet Frost had never been fond of the cold. In fact, she outright despised it. She tugged the thick woolen scarf tighter around her neck as the snow-crusted landscape of the Arctic Circle stretched out before her, an endless expanse of white beneath a bruised sky. Her breath billowed in front of her, tiny clouds disappearing into the frigid air. The driver, who hadn't said more than two words since picking her up at the tiny airport, glanced at her through the rearview mirror as they crested a hill. His eyes twinkled, perhaps from amusement, perhaps from some Arctic madness Violet couldn't quite grasp.

"THERE IT IS," he said gruffly, his voice muffled by the thick layers of scarves and hats he wore. Violet followed his gaze out the frost-rimmed window.

THE ICE HOTEL rose out of the tundra like a crystal palace from some forgotten fairy tale. Its towering, translucent walls shimmered in the pale Arctic light, the entire structure seeming to glow with an ethereal blue hue, as if it were sculpted from the sky itself. Glittering ice spires spiraled up toward the heavens, and intricate carvings adorned the frozen facade—reindeer, wolves, and other creatures native to this unforgiving land. Every angle reflected light in a kaleidoscope of shifting colors.

Even through her distaste for the cold, Violet couldn't help but be impressed.

As the car pulled to a stop, she wrapped her fingers—clad in fuzzy mittens—around the handle of her bag and stepped out onto the snow-packed path. Immediately, the cold bit into her like a swarm of tiny, icy daggers. A shiver crept up her spine, not just from the temperature, but from the strange feeling that always accompanied her when she arrived somewhere new. The emotions of the place swirled around her in waves of color and sound, too subtle for anyone else to notice but impossible for her to ignore.

Synesthesia. It was both her greatest gift and her biggest curse. Emotions had a way of manifesting themselves through hues and tones no one else could see. Joy rang like delicate bells in soft pinks, while deceit glinted in jagged shards of yellow. Fear—Violet knew fear well—hummed in deep, vibrating reds.

As she trudged toward the hotel entrance, the cold already seeping through her boots, she tried to push back the synesthetic storm that came with this place. The icy grandeur of the hotel radiated a chorus of cold, sharp notes, underscored by the occasional pulse of something darker, something lurking beneath the polished surface. She wasn't sure if it was the hotel itself or the people inside.

The grand ice doors opened with a soft creak, and she was immediately met by a burst of warmth—well, relative warmth—emanating from within. A bellhop, tall and slender with a smile as frozen as the sculptures around him, greeted her and offered to take her coat. Violet held onto it a second longer than necessary, reluctant to part with any layer of warmth. The bellhop's smile flickered, but he didn't comment. Instead, he gestured for her to follow him through the shimmering ice corridors.

It was all as opulent as the bride-to-be had promised. The walls were lined with sculptures that seemed almost alive—crystal-clear ice wolves frozen mid-howl, swirling shapes that twisted like icy winds caught in motion, chandeliers that glittered overhead like frost-kissed diamonds. It was extravagant, sure, but beneath the beauty, Violet sensed something else, something a little too pristine.

She pulled out her phone, the screen lighting up with the message that had brought her here in the first place:

"Violet, I need your help. Please come to the Ice Hotel as soon as you can. My wedding is in three days, and I'm terrified something terrible is going to happen. The necklace—it's irreplaceable. If anything goes wrong... I can't even think about it. I'll pay

whatever you need. Please. We'll talk when you arrive."

—Sophia

The bride-to-be, Sophia Verlaine, was no stranger to luxury. Her name alone conjured images of old money and high society. But Violet knew all too well that wealth didn't protect people from fear. If anything, it made them more vulnerable to it.

Sophia's prized possession, a priceless diamond necklace, was the centerpiece of her lavish winter wedding. The necklace had a history as frosty as the Arctic winds—a gift passed down through generations, once owned by royalty, now worth more than most people could imagine. Sophia wasn't just scared of losing a valuable piece of jewelry. She was scared of losing a part of herself, her legacy.

Violet couldn't afford to say no. Business had been slow, and while she hated the idea of spending the next few days in an icebox, she needed the money. And if there was one thing Violet Frost was good at, it was solving mysteries, no matter how bizarre or chilly.

As she followed the bellhop deeper into the heart of the hotel, she felt the familiar flickers of emotion rise around her. Something wasn't right here. The colors shifted in the corners of her vision—faint tendrils of distrust curling around the edges, the faint hum of anxiety vibrating in the air like a low drone.

. . .

THE NECKLACE MIGHT NOT BE the only thing in danger.

WITH A SIGH, Violet pulled her scarf up higher, already feeling the chill in her bones. The Ice Hotel was magnificent, yes, but it was also a maze of secrets waiting to be uncovered. And with the kind of guests Sophia had likely invited to her high-society wedding, Violet knew this case was going to be anything but straightforward.

SHE JUST HOPED she could figure it all out before she froze.

Cold Comfort

Violet Frost stood in the glittering ballroom of the Ice Hotel, her breath puffing out in little clouds as she glanced around at the eclectic group of people gathered for the wedding. It was hard to focus with the constant low hum of her synesthesia buzzing in her senses—emotions bouncing off people in bursts of color and sound. Despite her best efforts to maintain composure, the chill seeping through her wool coat and the odd mix of personalities in the room made her feel even more out of place.

She hadn't met the bride yet, but she could spot Sophia Verlaine from across the room. The bride-to-be was pacing near the massive ice sculpture that dominated the center of the ballroom—a reindeer frozen mid-leap, crystalline antlers reaching toward the ceiling. Sophia was the epitome of wealthy socialite perfection: tall, slender, with immaculate blonde curls pinned to one side. But the frantic purple haze swirling around her in Violet's synesthetic perception told a different story. Sophia was a bundle of nerves.

. . .

The bellhop who had guided her inside, now standing by the door, whispered in her ear, "The bride has been waiting for you. She's a bit... on edge."

Violet gave a small nod and squared her shoulders, making her way across the ballroom. Her attention, however, was quickly pulled away by a voice—booming, theatrical, and with just the slightest Nordic accent.

"Ah! You must be the detective!" the man shouted, arms outstretched in a dramatic gesture. His chef's coat was as immaculate as it was oversized, and the name embroidered on the chest read *Bjorn*. The man beamed as though Violet were a long-lost friend rather than a stranger intruding on his icy kingdom.

Violet tilted her head. "I'm Violet Frost," she said, unsure how to respond to such exuberance. "You're... the chef?"

"Chef Bjorn!" He grabbed her hand in an enthusiastic grip, his meaty fingers almost swallowing hers. "Master of reindeer cuisine, creator of delicacies that make the soul *sing*." He smiled wide, his teeth bright against his ruddy face. "I hope you enjoy what I've prepared for the wedding feast. Everything—*everything*—will feature reindeer. It's all part of the Arctic experience!" His eyes sparkled, though Violet couldn't help but notice a strange gray tint swirling around him—an almost feverish enthusiasm that felt off-kilter. His passion for reindeer bordered on obsession.

. . .

Frost & Found: A Winter Mystery at the Ice Hotel

VIOLET BLINKED. "SOUNDS... INTERESTING."

BJORN CLAPPED HIS HANDS. "Interesting? No, no, no! *Life-changing!*" He turned and marched back toward the grand dining table, his voice still booming as he issued instructions to the waitstaff. Violet couldn't help but feel a twinge of discomfort as she watched him go. Passion was one thing, but Bjorn's energy hummed with something a bit too intense.

"VIOLET!"

SOPHIA'S VOICE WAS SHARP, cutting through Violet's thoughts. She turned to see the bride hurrying toward her, her expensive heels tapping rapidly against the ice floor. The purples around her deepened, flickering with anxiety.

"I'M SO GLAD you're here," Sophia said, her breath coming in short, stressed bursts. "It's been chaos—absolute chaos. I haven't slept in days. Everyone's been asking about the necklace, and I—" She stopped, her eyes wide as she glanced around nervously. "I just need to know it's safe."

Violet nodded, her tone calm. "That's why I'm here. Have you noticed anything suspicious?"

"NOT YET," Sophia whispered, fidgeting with the lace on her dress. "But the guests... they're all so *strange*. I don't trust anyone." She lowered her voice even more. "Especially *him*." She jerked her chin toward a man standing near the bar, his dark coat blending into the ice-covered wall behind him.

Violet followed her gaze. The man looked about forty, tall and slender with sharp features, his expression unreadable. His eyes were fixed on a glass of something amber-colored, which he swirled slowly in his hand. The colors around him were muted, as if he were holding something back.

"Who is that?" Violet asked.

"That's Alden Graves," Sophia replied, her voice taut. "He's a poet—well, *calls* himself a poet, though I've never understood half of what he says. He only speaks in riddles. And he's been... hovering. Always nearby. I don't like it." She shivered, pulling her coat closer around her shoulders.

Violet studied Alden for a moment, then nodded. "I'll keep an eye on him. Just try to stay calm. I'll make sure everything's under control."

Sophia didn't look convinced, but she gave a tight smile. "Thank you. I'm just... I'm so nervous. The necklace is irreplaceable. And without it, the wedding—" She cut herself off and shook her head, her voice trembling. "It's not just a necklace. It's everything."

Violet was about to ask more when a sharp cry pierced the air. Both women spun around to see a commotion near the front of the ballroom. Two guests were gesturing wildly toward the coatroom, where a young woman in hotel staff uniform stood, her face pale and her hands shaking.

"What's going on?" Violet asked, already striding toward the scene.

The young woman, clearly in shock, stammered as the words spilled out. "The necklace... it's gone."

For a second, the room seemed to freeze. Violet's heart sank as she exchanged a look with Sophia, whose face had turned as white as the ice surrounding them.

"Are you sure?" Violet asked, keeping her voice steady despite the sudden tension crackling through the air.

The staff member nodded vigorously, tears welling in her eyes. "I went to check on it, just like I was told. It was in the safe—locked and secure. But when I opened it, the necklace was... it was gone!"

Sophia gasped, clutching Violet's arm. "No. No, this can't be happening."

Violet's mind raced. The hotel was isolated. No one could leave without being noticed, which meant that the thief had to be someone still here, among the guests and staff.

"Everyone," Violet called out, raising her voice. "Please stay calm. No one will be allowed to leave until we find the necklace."

The room buzzed with a rising chorus of murmurs and whispers, suspicion hanging thick in the air. Violet's synesthesia was in overdrive—colors flashing, emotions swirling. Anxiety was sharp in jagged streaks of yellow, while nervous reds pulsed from several of the guests.

. . .

She turned back to Sophia. "It's time for me to get to work."

As the bride nodded, tears glistening in her eyes, Violet took a deep breath. The cold was no longer her only worry. Somewhere in this frozen paradise, someone had just made a dangerous move.

And Violet Frost was going to find them.

Eccentric Suspects

Violet Frost adjusted her scarf as she sat in a small, ice-carved alcove just off the main ballroom, where she had set up her temporary investigation headquarters. The Ice Hotel's cold blue walls reflected the dancing lights of the ballroom's chandeliers, casting flickers of shadow and light in a way that made everything feel a little too surreal. She'd seen her fair share of odd crime scenes, but this place felt like something out of a fever dream—glittering ice, eccentric guests, and a stolen necklace worth more than most people made in a lifetime.

One by one, the guests trickled in for their interviews, each more peculiar than the last. As they entered, Violet's senses sharpened, her synesthesia making every interaction vivid, emotional, and, often, overwhelming. The colors, sounds, and even faint tastes that accompanied the guests were as varied as their personalities, and each clue felt like it was hidden behind a veil she needed to pull back.

. . .

Her first interviewee was Alden Graves, the cryptic poet Sophia had pointed out earlier. He entered the alcove with an air of studied detachment, his thin lips curved into a barely-there smile. He wore a long black coat, the collar pulled high, and his dark hair fell into his eyes, which flicked around the room as though evaluating its aesthetic worth rather than the purpose of his presence.

Alden sat down across from Violet and steepled his fingers. "Ah, the inquisitor arrives," he said, his voice smooth and melodic, but with an unsettling edge. "To unweave the webs that bind the stars."

Violet resisted the urge to sigh. She had dealt with poets before, and they all loved their cryptic nonsense. But Alden was different; his words felt almost rehearsed, and the colors swirling around him were complex—a mix of deep blue melancholy with splashes of dark green, the color of envy, creeping in at the edges.

"I'm not here for the stars," Violet replied dryly, her breath puffing in the cold air. "I'm here for the necklace. Can you tell me where you were around the time it disappeared?"

Alden tilted his head, his smile growing. "Time is a fickle mistress, don't you think? One minute it's there, the next—poof—vanished into the wind like a dream. But if you must know, I was... composing. Reflecting upon the frozen beauty of our surroundings. Ice has a way of capturing the soul, don't you think?" His eyes sparkled, but Violet caught the glint of something else—a pale yellow note of dishonesty.

. . .

"Composing, was it?" Violet asked, her tone even. "Did anyone see you?"

Alden's smile faltered for a split second before returning, and this time the colors around him shifted—a sharp flicker of red, like the sound of a string snapping. Anxiety.

"No," he said finally. "I prefer solitude when I work."

Violet leaned forward. "And your thoughts on the necklace? You seem like someone who might appreciate its beauty."

Alden's eyes narrowed, but he held her gaze. "Beauty lies in the eye, but I prefer the beauty of creation to the weight of material things. The necklace is lovely, yes, but it is only a thing. What matters is the story it tells."

The words came out smoothly, but they rang hollow in Violet's mind. There was something about the way he spoke of the necklace that felt off—a discordant note in the otherwise fluid melody of his speech. She couldn't pinpoint it yet, but her synesthesia told her to keep him in mind.

After Alden left, Violet jotted down a few notes before the next guest arrived—a man who could not have been more different.

Eirik Halvorsen strode into the alcove with the swagger of someone who was used to getting what he wanted. The tech billionaire, whose fortune was built on cutting-edge virtual reality and artificial intelligence, was dressed impeccably in a tailored parka, his platinum blond hair swept back in a way that made him look like a Nordic prince. He sat down without waiting for Violet's invitation, his pale blue eyes locking onto hers with unnerving intensity.

. . .

"Let's get this over with," he said, his voice clipped, as if he were annoyed at having to waste time on such trivial matters. "I have important business to attend to."

Violet didn't flinch. She'd dealt with his type before—people so wealthy they assumed the world revolved around them. "I'm sure you do," she said, her voice steady. "But I need to ask you some questions about the necklace."

Eirik waved a hand dismissively. "I don't care about that necklace. Do you know how many priceless artifacts I have in my private collection? One more or less doesn't matter to me."

Violet raised an eyebrow. His words were confident, but the moment he mentioned his collection, she noticed a faint buzz in the air—a barely audible hum, like static crackling just beneath the surface. It was the sound she often heard when someone was hiding something. The colors around him were a cold, flat blue with streaks of silver, which told her he was trying hard to maintain control, but there was something unsettled underneath it all.

"You seem knowledgeable about valuable items," Violet said, watching his reaction carefully. "How would someone go about stealing a necklace like that?"

Eirik's eyes flickered for a brief second, but his expression remained calm. "I wouldn't know. I deal in technology, not petty theft." His voice was laced with arrogance, but there was a flash of red-orange—defensiveness.

"Is that so?" Violet asked, her tone light. "You haven't noticed anyone acting suspiciously? Or perhaps you've heard something?"

. . .

Eirik leaned back in his chair, crossing his arms. "This is a waste of time. If someone took the necklace, it's not my problem. I'd suggest you look elsewhere, detective."

Violet gave a thin smile. "I intend to."

When Eirik left, the room felt noticeably calmer, as if the tension he brought with him had finally dissipated. Violet frowned. Both Alden and Eirik were hiding something, but neither had given her enough to go on yet. She still needed more pieces to fit together.

Next up was Marla Raines, a woman who immediately struck Violet as both charming and dangerous in equal measure. Marla was dressed in head-to-toe faux fur, her auburn hair falling in perfect waves over her shoulders. She carried herself like a woman who knew how to manipulate a room. As she sat down, her perfume—something sweet and overpowering—filled the air, making Violet's senses buzz with cloying floral notes.

"So," Marla began, her voice smooth as silk, "I hear you're the one trying to find that poor missing necklace. Such a shame, isn't it?"

"That's what I'm here for," Violet replied. "Can you tell me where you were when it disappeared?"

Marla smiled coyly, leaning in slightly. "Oh, darling, I was having the most delightful conversation with Chef Bjorn about his... shall we say... *unique* menu. You know how obsessed he is with those poor reindeer, don't you?"

Violet noted the amusement in her voice, but something about the way Marla said "obsessed" made the hairs on the back of her neck stand up. Marla was enjoying this too much—the mystery, the chaos, the attention. And as she spoke, the colors around her were slippery, shifting from light, playful pinks to deeper, more sinister shades of purple.

"Tell me, Marla," Violet said casually, "what's your interest in the necklace?"

"Oh, none at all," Marla said, waving her hand. "Jewellery has never been my thing. I much prefer… experiences." She smiled, but Violet sensed a dissonant note in her response—a faint, metallic tang, like copper on the tongue.

She was lying.

Violet couldn't quite figure out why, but Marla's reaction to the necklace had felt strange, off-kilter in a way that made her uneasy. She noted the feeling, tucking it away for later, knowing it could be important.

As the day went on, Violet continued to interview the guests and staff, each more peculiar than the last. A waiter with a penchant for eavesdropping, a wedding guest who seemed overly interested in Nordic mythology, and a hotel manager who couldn't stop fidgeting with his tie—all of them gave Violet something to think about, but none gave her the breakthrough she needed.

Yet there was something undeniable building beneath the surface, a cacophony of colors, sounds, and sensations that told Violet she was close to finding something important. One of them knew more than they were letting on.

And soon, she would uncover what it was.

The Frozen Body

The Frozen BodyViolet stepped out into the biting cold of the hotel courtyard, the night air sharp as glass against her skin. The northern lights shimmered faintly overhead, casting the snow-covered landscape in ghostly shades of green and blue. The Ice Hotel's courtyard was eerily quiet, the wind whispering through the towering ice sculptures like secrets meant only for the Arctic night. But what lay beneath one of those sculptures was no secret.

The body was sprawled beneath a massive snow sculpture of a reindeer, its antlers twisting elegantly toward the sky. The frozen form was covered in a fine layer of frost, making the face almost unrecognisable, but the outline of the body was unmistakable—a guest, frozen solid in the snow.

Violet's breath caught in her throat. The whimsical, quirky air of the Ice Hotel that had previously amused her was gone, replaced by a creeping sense of dread.

. . .

The stolen necklace had been bad enough, but now there was a body, and everything about the situation shifted. The stakes were higher, and whoever had taken the necklace might have done much worse than a simple theft.

She knelt carefully next to the body, the cold seeping through her gloves as she reached out to examine the scene. The man's face was contorted in a frozen grimace, his features locked in a rictus of fear or pain. His hands were splayed out, clutching at the snow beneath him as if he'd tried to claw his way free. Violet's synesthesia kicked in, the colors and sensations around the body flickering in her mind—a strange mix of pale blue sadness, deep red fear, and a low, thrumming sound that felt like distant thunder.

"Who found him?" Violet asked, her voice sharper than she intended.

"One of the staff," came the reply. It was the hotel manager, a nervous man named Karl who had been hovering near the scene since Violet had arrived. His hands fidgeted constantly, adjusting his coat, then his hat, then back to his coat. "She was clearing snow off the sculptures and found him just lying there."

Violet nodded, her eyes sweeping over the scene. The courtyard was lined with other ice and snow sculptures—some whimsical, others more abstract—but none gave off the same dark energy as this one. She could feel something wrong here, something deeply off. The body hadn't been there long; the frost was fresh, the snow not fully settled over him. Whoever had left him here had done it recently, and they hadn't expected him to be found so soon.

"Who is he?" Violet asked, turning to Karl.

"That's... that's Mr. Alden Graves," Karl stammered, clearly shaken. "The poet. You met him yesterday."

Violet's heart sank. Alden had been strange, cryptic even, but murder? That felt too extreme for the quiet, riddle-spinning man she had interviewed. And yet, here he was—frozen solid under a snow sculpture, in a place where no one was supposed to be.

"Who else knows about this?" Violet asked, her mind racing as she stood up, brushing the snow from her gloves.

"Only a few staff members. We haven't told the other guests yet," Karl replied, wringing his hands. "We didn't want to cause a panic."

"Good," Violet said. "Keep it that way for now. The last thing we need is hysteria."

She took a deep breath and forced herself to focus. First, the necklace. Now, a body. Were they connected? Had Alden known something that got him killed? Or had this been a crime of opportunity, with the murderer thinking they could use the chaotic atmosphere of the missing necklace to cover their tracks?

Violet wasn't sure, but she knew one thing: this wasn't a simple theft anymore. She had a murder to solve.

Back inside the hotel, the atmosphere had shifted. Though the other guests didn't yet know about Alden's death, there was an undercurrent of tension in the air that hadn't been there before. Violet could feel it, like the low hum of static just out of earshot. People were anxious, suspicious, and more guarded than they had been when she'd first arrived. Her synesthesia heightened the experience, the colors around the guests darker now, more muddled—reds of anxiety, purples of fear, and a sharp yellow note of deceit that lingered in the air.

She needed to talk to the guests again, to feel out their reactions to Alden's death. She didn't have the luxury of subtlety anymore—there was no time for it. She had to find out what these people knew before anyone else ended up beneath the snow.

Her first stop was Sophia, who was sitting near the grand ice bar, her fingers trembling as she sipped a glass of champagne. The vibrant purple of her earlier anxiety had deepened into a dark bruise-like shade, and the faint silvery tint of guilt lingered around her, though Violet wasn't sure why.

"Sophia," Violet said, taking a seat beside her. "I need to ask you something, and I need you to be completely honest with me."

Sophia looked up, her eyes wide and tearful. "What is it? Is this about the necklace?"

Violet hesitated for a moment, then nodded. "Partly. Do you know anything about Alden Graves?"

Sophia frowned, her hand clenching around her glass. "Alden? He's... well, he was odd. He spoke in riddles and made people uncomfortable. But I wouldn't say I *knew* him. He was just another guest. Why?"

Violet studied her face, watching the colors flicker around her—nervous shades of blue and purple, but nothing sharp, nothing that screamed guilt. "Alden was found dead outside," she said quietly.

Sophia's glass slipped from her hand, shattering on the ice floor. "Dead? How...?"

"We're still figuring that out. But I need you to think. Did Alden say anything to you that might have seemed strange? Did he mention the necklace or anyone acting suspiciously?"

Sophia shook her head, her face pale. "No. I mean, he was always strange, but... no. I didn't speak to him much." She paused, then added, "He did seem interested in the necklace, though. He asked about it a few times, almost as if it fascinated him. But I didn't think anything of it at the time."

Violet nodded, tucking the information away. Alden had been interested in the necklace. That wasn't much, but it was something. Perhaps whoever had taken the necklace had also taken Alden's life when he got too close to the truth.

Violet left Sophia, her mind racing. As she moved through the hotel's glittering ice halls, her senses began to sharpen, the colors and sounds swirling in a dizzying symphony around her.

Something was off, but she couldn't quite put her finger on it. The atmosphere was thick with tension, and she could feel the lies slipping through conversations like shadows.

As she stepped back outside to the courtyard for another look, the icy wind whipped at her face. The snow had settled more since she had first found Alden, but something drew her back to the reindeer sculpture, its frozen form gleaming under the starlight.

Her eyes drifted toward the base of the sculpture, where the snow had been disturbed. And that's when she saw it—something barely visible against the pristine white snow. Violet knelt down, brushing the snow aside, and found a small, torn piece of fabric snagged on the edge of the reindeer's leg. It was dark, almost black, and felt expensive to the touch.

As she examined the fabric, her synesthesia flared up. The colors around the sculpture shifted—blurry at first, then clearer. A sound began to resonate in her mind, faint but distinct: muffled footsteps crunching through the snow. It was as if her senses were picking up an echo from the night before, replaying the scene like a distant memory.

Someone had been here recently—someone who had tried to cover their tracks but had missed this small detail. Violet could almost hear the rapid breathing, feel the panic in the air. Whoever had left the torn fabric had been in a hurry. And now she had a clue—a clue that could link the theft of the necklace and Alden's murder.

She stood up, clutching the fabric in her hand, her mind buzzing with possibilities. Someone had been near this sculpture last night, and they hadn't just been admiring the ice art.

They had been covering up a crime.

As the night wore on, Violet's head swam with half-truths, evasions, and cryptic warnings. She had multiple mysteries on her hands now—the stolen necklace, the frozen body, and the strange behaviour of everyone around her. Her synesthesia buzzed with chaotic colors and sounds, each one clashing with the next, making it hard to focus on the truth hidden beneath the surface.

Alden's death wasn't an accident. Someone had killed him, and that same someone had taken the necklace. The torn fabric was her first solid lead, and it was only a matter of time before she connected the dots.

The Ice Hotel held too many secrets, and Violet was getting closer to the truth. But the deeper she dug, the more dangerous this frozen paradise became.

One thing was certain: the killer hadn't finished yet.

An Icy Labyrinth

An Icy LabyrinthViolet Frost stood at the entrance to yet another icy corridor, her breath clouding the air in front of her. The Ice Hotel was a dazzling labyrinth, every hallway more intricate and ornate than the last. The place was enchanting, sure, but Violet was starting to realise that its beauty served as the perfect cover for secrets—secrets buried deep within the frozen walls.

She had spent hours wandering the hotel, following leads, questioning guests and staff, but the further she went, the more lost she felt—both literally and metaphorically. Every turn led to another corridor of shimmering ice sculptures, rooms that blurred together in their opulence. The grandeur was almost disorienting. Violet's sense of direction, usually sharp, was beginning to fail her in the maze of polished ice and snow. The hotel itself felt alive, twisting and turning in ways that made her question whether the walls were shifting when she wasn't looking.

. . .

As she walked, her mind hummed with fragments of her investigation. Alden's body, frozen beneath the snow sculpture, the missing necklace, the cryptic words of the guests—each clue floated just out of reach, tantalising but incomplete. And then there was the torn fabric, the faint echoes of footsteps that her synesthesia had picked up near Alden's body. They kept replaying in her mind, like a piece of music she couldn't stop hearing.

Turning a corner, she found herself in a new space: an ice bar. Carved entirely out of gleaming crystal-like ice, the bar was illuminated by flickering blue and purple lights. Ice stools were arranged in front of the bar, while delicate sculptures of arctic animals adorned the walls. The cold here was more intense than in other parts of the hotel, biting into her through her layers of clothing. Her boots crunched on the packed snow floor as she moved deeper into the room, taking in the ornate details.

It was beautiful, but Violet had learned that beauty here often masked something darker.

As she moved through the bar, her senses heightened, the faint sounds of a hushed conversation caught her attention. Her synesthesia flared up, the vibrations of the voices humming through the walls in faint yellow tones. She followed the sound, moving quietly past the frozen tables and chairs until she came to a secluded corner near the back.

Two staff members stood just beyond the bar's edge, their voices low but tense.

"I'm telling you, we need to keep quiet about this," one of them said, a sharp note of fear in his voice. "If anyone finds out what's been happening, it'll be our jobs."

The other staff member, a woman with a strained expression, hissed back, "We've already lost control of the situation! Alden is dead, for God's sake. This isn't just about the necklace anymore. If anyone finds out we knew..."

VIOLET LEANED IN CLOSER, trying to pick up more, her heart pounding as the colors around her shifted into anxious reds. The words confirmed what she had suspected—there was more going on behind the scenes than anyone was letting on. The staff knew something, and they were desperate to keep it hidden.

The male staff member glanced around nervously. "I'm just saying, we need to play it smart. There's too much at stake here. The management will have our heads if this gets out."

THE WOMAN SHOOK HER HEAD, her voice dropping even lower. "You're right. We'll keep it quiet for now. But we need to stay alert. Someone's already gotten too close. And if they find out about the tunnels—"

Before she could finish, Violet's foot shifted on the snow, making a faint crunching sound. Both staff members whipped around, their eyes wide with panic. Violet froze, quickly stepping back into the shadows. The two exchanged a glance, and without another word, they rushed off down a side corridor, disappearing into the maze of ice.

VIOLET STOOD STILL, her mind racing. *Tunnels.* They had mentioned tunnels. And something about losing control of the situation. The necklace, the murder, the missing pieces—everything seemed to converge around this hidden secret.

Violet knew she had to find out more. Her instincts—and her synesthesia—buzzed with urgency. The staff were hiding something, and whatever it was, it had to be connected to the crimes.

As she continued through the hotel's labyrinthine halls, Violet's attention was drawn to a new section she hadn't explored yet. The walls here were carved with intricate designs, ice sculptures depicting ancient Nordic symbols and folklore. The temperature seemed to drop further as she ventured deeper, the cold becoming almost oppressive. Her breath crystallised in the air, and her boots slipped slightly on the icy floor.

The corridor opened up into a ballroom, its walls and ceiling made entirely of ice. Crystal chandeliers hung above, and frozen figures danced in elegant poses across the room, their forms sculpted with such detail that they almost seemed alive. Violet stood in awe for a moment, taking in the grandeur of it all. But something about the room felt wrong. It was too quiet. Too perfect.

Her synesthesia began to stir, a soft hum rising in the back of her mind, the colors shifting into pale blues and greens. The feeling pulled her toward the far corner of the room, where the ice seemed to glisten in a way that was different from the rest of the room. She moved closer, running her hand along the surface of the wall.

. . .

And then, she felt it—a subtle vibration. The sound that followed was faint, almost imperceptible, but her heightened senses picked it up clearly. A low, rhythmic tapping, like footsteps on the other side of the wall.

Violet pressed her ear against the ice, and the sound became clearer. Someone was moving behind the walls.

A hidden tunnel.

Her pulse quickened as she traced her hand along the wall, looking for any sort of mechanism or clue. After a moment, her fingers brushed against a small indentation—almost invisible in the ice. She pushed on it gently, and with a soft *click*, a panel of the ice wall slid open, revealing a narrow, icy passage leading downward into the depths of the hotel.

Without hesitation, Violet slipped through the opening, her breath coming in short, visible puffs as she descended the slippery steps into the tunnel below.

The tunnel was colder than anywhere else in the hotel. The air felt heavier, almost suffocating, as Violet moved deeper underground. The walls of the passage were rougher here, not as polished or ornate as the rest of the hotel. It felt hidden, forgotten —exactly the kind of place where someone would stash something they didn't want found.

Her synesthesia began to hum louder, the colors in the tunnel swirling in muted browns and gray's. Anxiety crept up her spine, the feeling of being watched gnawing at the back of her mind. She followed the tunnel, her flashlight cutting through the darkness as she moved deeper into the hidden passage.

. . .

AT THE END of the tunnel, she came to a small, concealed room, carved roughly from the ice. It was cramped, barely big enough to stand in, but what caught her attention wasn't the room itself—it was what was inside.

A STASH.

Piled high in the corner of the room were valuable items: watches, jewelry, bags—possessions from the hotel's guests. Some of the items still had tags attached, their luxury brands glittering under the faint light. And there, tucked under a pile of scarves and coats, was something else—a small, ornate box, intricately carved and gleaming with silver.

Violet reached for it, her breath catching in her throat. She opened the box slowly, her fingers trembling from both the cold and anticipation.

INSIDE, nestled in velvet, was a sparkling diamond necklace. The necklace. Sophia's missing treasure.

Violet exhaled, the weight of the discovery sinking in. But this was far from over. She had found the necklace, but now she had even more questions. Who had hidden it here? And why were all these other items stashed away in this secret tunnel?

THE SOUND of faint footsteps echoed down the tunnel, snapping her back to reality. Someone was coming.

Violet quickly tucked the necklace back into the box and backed away from the stash. Her heart pounded as she looked for a way out, her mind racing. She had uncovered a hidden part of the

Ice Hotel—now she just had to get out of it before she became its next victim.

As she turned to leave, the footsteps grew louder.

Cold Hearts

Violet Frost sat in the ice bar, her breath clouding the air as she reviewed the events of the last few days. The once whimsical hotel had turned darker, its grandeur a thin veil over growing tension.

The wedding guests, who had arrived with excitement and anticipation, now moved through the frozen halls with suspicion in their eyes. She could feel it with every conversation—jealousy, greed, and betrayal simmering beneath the surface. Her synesthesia buzzed relentlessly, the colors in the hotel turning muddier and more intense as the tangled web of motives started to take shape in her mind.

Alden Graves' murder had shocked everyone, but it was clear to Violet that the dead poet wasn't the only target. The missing necklace had been found in the hidden tunnel beneath the ice, surrounded by other stolen items, yet it still didn't explain why Alden had been killed. She couldn't shake the feeling that there was more to it, a bigger scheme that tied everything together. Her instincts told her she was close, but the final pieces of the puzzle still eluded her.

. . .

THE TENSION among the guests had been palpable all morning. As Violet moved through the ballroom, she noticed the subtle glances exchanged between certain individuals—the way a few guests avoided eye contact or whispered behind each other's backs. Her synesthesia heightened her awareness of their emotions, painting the air with swirling hues of yellow distrust and deep green envy. It was almost overwhelming.

SHE PAUSED BY A WINDOW, looking out at the snow-covered courtyard where Alden's body had been found. The reindeer sculpture loomed eerily in the distance. The image reminded her of the torn fabric and the muffled footsteps she had discovered—small pieces of evidence that still felt disconnected.

WHY KILL ALDEN? And why hide the necklace only to leave clues that led to its discovery? Violet's mind raced, replaying the hushed conversation she had overheard between the staff. There was fear there, but fear of what?

Her thoughts were interrupted by the sound of clinking glasses and raised voices coming from the dining room. She straightened, her senses immediately sharpening. Something was wrong.

WHEN VIOLET ENTERED the dining room, she was greeted by the overwhelming scent of Bjorn's latest culinary creation: a lavish feast centered, once again, around his obsession—reindeer-themed cuisine. The guests were seated at the long ice table, looking uncomfortable and tense. Bjorn himself stood proudly at the head of the room, his chest puffed out as he presented the meal.

. . .

But something was off.

One of the guests, a woman named Clara, who had been particularly vocal about her distaste for Bjorn's unusual dishes, was slumped in her chair, her face pale, her eyes half-closed. A low murmur spread through the room as the other guests began to notice.

"Clara?" someone called out, but she didn't respond.

Violet's heart quickened as she pushed through the crowd, reaching Clara's side just as her glass slipped from her hand and shattered on the ice floor.

"Get her some help!" Violet shouted, but even before anyone could move, her synesthesia flared to life. The colors around Clara shimmered in frantic swirls of sickly green and sharp, jagged orange. Poison.

Bjorn's face went white as the guests began to panic. "I-I don't understand," he stammered, his voice rising with fear. "It was just a normal dish! Reindeer stew, like the others! There's no way—"

Violet's mind raced as she looked around the table. Clara wasn't the type to take risks, especially with food she had already voiced her discomfort with. This wasn't an accident. Someone had tampered with the dish, and it had nearly killed her.

. . .

Within minutes, the hotel's small medical staff rushed in to tend to Clara, whisking her away to another room for observation. The guests huddled together, whispering in fearful tones. Violet stayed back, watching their reactions carefully, her synesthesia helping her separate true concern from hidden malice.

Bjorn hovered at the side, wringing his hands, his usually bombastic demeanor deflated. His vibrant personality had been dulled to a muted gray of guilt and confusion.

"She's going to be alright," one of the medics said as they returned to the room, "but she was definitely poisoned. Not enough to kill her, but she was lucky."

A wave of murmurs spread through the room, and Violet caught the words *sabotage* and *revenge* more than once.

Violet's mind snapped back into gear. The attempted poisoning wasn't random. It had to be connected to the necklace, to Alden's murder, and perhaps to something even deeper. The threads of jealousy and betrayal that had been weaving through the wedding party were starting to tighten.

She turned to Bjorn, whose face had lost its usual ruddy glow. "You were in charge of the meal," she said quietly but firmly. "Did anyone else have access to the kitchen?"

Bjorn shook his head, still trembling. "No one. I was there the whole time. No one else touched the food. I swear!"

Violet looked around the room, scanning the faces of the guests. Some were pale with shock, others glancing nervously at each other. But one guest in particular caught her attention. Eirik Halvorsen, the tech billionaire with a deep obsession for Nordic folklore, stood near the back of the room, watching the scene with a detached air. He hadn't rushed forward like the others. In fact, he had barely reacted.

Violet's eyes narrowed. Eirik had been unusually calm throughout the investigation, and now, his indifference felt almost calculated.

LATER THAT EVENING, Violet wandered the icy halls again, her mind swirling with everything that had happened. She had a feeling that Clara wasn't the intended target of the poisoning, but rather, an unfortunate victim of someone else's grander scheme. Whoever was behind this wanted to create fear and chaos, and they were succeeding.

AS SHE APPROACHED the ballroom again, her synesthesia flared. A sharp, metallic sound hummed in her ears, and the colors around her vision intensified—reds and yellows flickering violently. Something was pulling her attention back to the reindeer sculpture outside.

Violet followed the feeling, stepping out into the cold night once again. The reindeer sculpture loomed ahead, its ice antlers catching the faint moonlight. She moved closer, kneeling near the base of the sculpture where Alden's body had been found.

AND THERE IT WAS.

A SMALL, almost invisible piece of evidence—caught in a crevice of the ice, barely noticeable against the snow. A tuft of fur. Reindeer fur, unmistakably clinging to the base of the sculpture. Violet carefully pulled it free, holding it up to the light.

Her mind flashed back to Bjorn's kitchen and the meals he had been serving all week. She remembered how meticulous he had been with his reindeer-themed dishes, using only imported ingredients. This fur, however, was too fresh, too real to have come from his supply.

VIOLET'S SYNESTHESIA BUZZED AGAIN, the colors around her sharpening with clarity. It wasn't just a culinary obsession at play here. The fur belonged to someone with an affinity for reindeer—a guest who had been too comfortable around the idea of reindeer-themed dishes, perhaps someone who had more than just a passing interest in Nordic folklore.

Her thoughts snapped back to Eirik.

EIRIK HAD BEEN FASCINATED by the idea of reindeer since the moment she met him. He had talked about it in passing, brushed it off as a cultural interest, but there had been an edge to his words. She remembered him mentioning how reindeer were central to many ancient Nordic traditions—traditions that sometimes involved sacrifice.

VIOLET FELT HER PULSE QUICKEN. The reindeer fur wasn't just a clue. It was a symbol. And if she was right, Eirik Halvorsen wasn't just an eccentric guest with a love for folklore. He was at the center of this tangled web, and whatever plan he had set into motion wasn't over yet.

. . .

As Violet stood there, clutching the fur, she knew she had to act quickly. Eirik's quiet demeanor and obsession with Nordic myths were hiding something far darker than she had imagined.

And the Ice Hotel was about to become the stage for his final, chilling act.

Warming Up to the Truth

Warming Up to the TruthViolet stood just outside the kitchen, her breath misting in front of her, steeling herself for what was coming. Bjorn, the Ice Hotel's celebrity chef, had become increasingly erratic since Clara's poisoning. His once larger-than-life persona was now fraying at the edges, his obsession with reindeer-themed dishes mutating into something more troubling. Violet had watched him spiral—his eyes wild, his hands trembling, the colors swirling around him with an unsettling intensity.

She pushed the door open and stepped inside, the warm air of the kitchen a welcome change from the biting cold of the hotel. Bjorn stood at the center of the chaos, barking orders at the kitchen staff as they rushed to prepare yet another extravagant meal. The heat from the stoves seemed to make him sweat even more than the pressure did. He looked up as Violet approached, his eyes narrowing.

. . .

"Ah, Detective Frost," he said, wiping his forehead with a cloth. "What brings you here? Come to criticize my cooking again?"

Violet kept her expression neutral. "I'm here to talk about the poisoning, Bjorn. Clara almost died. That wasn't just a cooking mistake."

Bjorn's face twisted into a defensive sneer, but Violet sensed more beneath it—his colors told her as much. The flashes of dull orange frustration mixed with erratic streaks of panic suggested he was hiding something. But the most important part? There was no deep red of malice, no dark hues of guilt that would indicate he had intended harm. Her synesthesia was telling her he was involved, but not in the way people thought.

"I didn't poison anyone," Bjorn snapped, his voice cracking slightly. "I've been preparing food my whole life. I know exactly what goes into every dish I make, and no one could have tampered with it without me knowing."

Violet tilted her head, watching the colors shift around him, the erratic energy buzzing in the air. "No one's saying you intentionally poisoned anyone," she said, keeping her tone calm but firm. "But something's changed in you since this wedding began. The dishes, the obsession with reindeer, the panic. It's all connected."

Bjorn's eyes flashed, and for a moment, Violet thought he might lash out. But then he slumped, the fight draining out of him. He pressed his hands against the counter, his knuckles turning white.

"I didn't want any of this," he muttered, his voice suddenly small. "This wedding, this ridiculous spectacle... I thought it would be good for my reputation. But everything's gone wrong." He looked up at her, his eyes wide and almost pleading. "I didn't kill anyone, Violet. I swear. But... I know more than I should."

The air around him shifted, and Violet's synesthesia hummed with a soft, silvery sound, signaling truth beneath the chaos.

"What do you know, Bjorn?" she asked quietly.

Bjorn hesitated, then glanced around as if afraid someone might overhear. "I saw something. The night before Alden was killed, someone was in the kitchen. They weren't supposed to be there. At first, I thought it was just one of the staff, but then I realized... they weren't taking food. They were hiding something." His hands shook as he gripped the counter. "They had the necklace."

Violet's heart skipped. "Who was it?"

Bjorn shook his head. "I didn't see their face. Just their silhouette. But they went into one of the service passageways."

The colors around him vibrated with fear and regret, but no deceit. He was telling the truth. He wasn't the killer, but he had seen something that could break the case wide open.

As Violet left the kitchen, her mind raced with Bjorn's revelation. The service passageways. It made sense now—how the necklace had been moved, how the stolen items had been hidden in the tunnels beneath the hotel. Someone had intimate knowledge of the hotel's layout, someone who could move through the labyrinth unnoticed.

. . .

Violet wandered the halls, her thoughts circling around the clues she had gathered, when she heard the soft shuffle of footsteps behind her. She turned to find one of the bellhops standing there—a young man with a slight frame and dark, expressive eyes that seemed to know more than they let on. He had been around since the beginning, always just in the background, silent but observant.

"Can I help you?" Violet asked, eyeing him carefully.

The bellhop gave a small smile, glancing around to make sure no one else was nearby. "Actually, I think I can help you," he said in a low voice.

Violet's curiosity piqued. "Go on."

He gestured for her to follow him, leading her down a series of narrow hallways that twisted deeper into the hotel. After several turns, he stopped in front of what appeared to be an unremarkable section of wall, then pushed a hidden panel, revealing a small passageway. The air inside was colder than ever, and Violet's breath caught in her throat as she stepped into the secret space.

"These passageways run through the entire hotel," the bellhop explained. "Most of the staff doesn't know about them, but I've been here long enough to figure them out. I think this is where you'll find the answers you're looking for."

He stepped back, allowing her to enter alone.

Violet nodded, her heart pounding. "Thank you."

The passage was narrow and winding, its icy walls slick beneath her gloved fingers. As she moved deeper, the sound of her footsteps echoed in the tight space. Her synesthesia was alive with faint whispers of sound and light, guiding her forward.

And then she heard it—a soft click behind her.

Before she could react, the passageway's door slammed shut, plunging her into icy darkness. Violet rushed back, pounding on the door, but it wouldn't budge. The temperature in the hidden room plummeted, the cold seeping into her bones. Someone had locked her in.

Betrayal.

Her heart raced as she realized the truth—someone she had trusted had led her into this trap. The bellhop, with his quiet demeanor and helpful information, had turned on her. But why? The cold around her intensified, and her mind began to blur as the temperature continued to drop.

She wouldn't last long in here. She had to find a way out.
Violet forced herself to stay calm, scanning the small room for anything she could use. The walls were smooth, but there were faint grooves in the ice—almost as if the passage had been carved by hand. She moved her fingers over the surface, feeling for any sign of weakness. Her breath came in shallow puffs as the cold bit into her, slowing her movements.

. . .

Then she found it—another hidden panel, smaller than the one the bellhop had shown her, concealed near the floor. She pressed it, and with a soft grinding sound, the wall shifted just enough to let her push it open.

Stumbling out into the corridor, she collapsed against the wall, her chest heaving. The air outside was still cold, but it was bearable compared to the icy tomb she had been trapped in. Violet stood slowly, her mind spinning. She had narrowly escaped, but now she knew just how close she was to the truth.

Someone inside the hotel was playing a dangerous game. They had the necklace, they had killed Alden, and they had tried to take her out before she could put all the pieces together.

But Violet wasn't done yet.

Shivering, she straightened, her survival instincts kicking in. She wasn't going to stop until she uncovered everything.

This wasn't just about a necklace anymore. It was about power, betrayal, and the dark secrets hidden within the Ice Hotel.

And now, she knew exactly where to look next.

The Ice Breaks

The Ice BreaksThe Ice Hotel was bathed in a soft, ethereal glow as the wedding day arrived. The tension in the air, however, was anything but serene. Violet Frost stood in the grand ballroom, her mind racing as she reviewed the evidence she had painstakingly collected. The stolen necklace, the torn fabric, the secret tunnel, the poisoned dish, and, of course, Alden Graves' frozen body—all the pieces of the puzzle were finally beginning to align. She could feel it, the truth swirling around her like the cold Arctic wind, just waiting for her to pull it all together.

Violet's synesthesia was in overdrive, colors flashing in her vision, emotions vibrating around her with every interaction she had. There was something deeply personal about this case, something tied to revenge, jealousy, and betrayal.

She sat down for a moment, laying out the clues in her mind. The torn fabric had been caught on the reindeer ice sculpture, where Alden's body had been found. It matched a gown worn by none other than the bride herself, Sophia Verlaine. That much had been clear from the start. But Sophia's apparent guilt wasn't adding up—she was too terrified of the events spiraling out of control to be the mastermind.

AND THEN THERE were the whispers she had overheard from the staff about the tunnels and hiding the necklace. The stolen items she'd discovered underground weren't just random—someone had been using those tunnels to move freely, stash stolen goods, and manipulate the events leading up to the wedding. But why? And how did Alden, the odd poet with a penchant for riddles, fit into all of this?

AS SHE PACED, Violet's thoughts returned to one critical point—the necklace. It had been moved, hidden in the tunnels, but who had the motive to steal it and why frame Alden? That was the key. *A personal vendetta.*

SUDDENLY, it clicked.

THE THEFT of the necklace and Alden's death weren't random acts. Alden had known something—something about the bride or someone close to her. The stolen necklace was a smokescreen, a cover for something far more personal. Alden had been in the wrong place at the wrong time, but he had seen too much. That's why he had to be silenced.

. . .

Violet's breath caught as the pieces fell into place. This wasn't just about the necklace. It was about revenge.

The jilted lover.

Her mind flashed back to Sophia's anxious glances toward one particular guest—the man she had tried to avoid since Violet had arrived. Frederick Langley, a former flame of Sophia, who had been invited to the wedding under the pretense of friendship but had harbored a grudge ever since their tumultuous breakup. Frederick had been calm, too calm, throughout the investigation, standing in the background, watching everything unfold with unsettling ease.

He had the knowledge of the hotel, the motive, and the connections. He had staged the theft of the necklace to ruin Sophia's wedding, framing Alden, who had been nosing around in his business. But things had spiraled out of control. Alden had found him, or worse, confronted him, and Frederick had panicked.

It all made sense now. But there was only one way to prove it.

The Ice Chapel was a masterpiece of frozen artistry, glittering like a crystalline cathedral under the Arctic sky. Guests were seated, their breath visible in the chilled air as they awaited the ceremony. The bride, Sophia, stood at the altar, her face pale but resolute. The tension among the guests was palpable, the events of the past few days casting a long shadow over what should have been a joyous occasion.

Violet stood at the back of the chapel, her pulse quickening. This was the moment. She had already informed the staff to keep a close eye on Frederick, and now, it was time for her to act.

As the ceremony began, Violet stepped forward, her voice ringing out through the icy silence. "I need to stop this," she said, her words freezing the room in place. All eyes turned toward her.

Sophia's eyes widened in shock. "What is this? What are you doing?"

"I'm sorry, Sophia," Violet said, her voice steady, "but the man responsible for everything that has happened—the missing necklace, Alden's death, and the chaos that has ensued—is here, at this very wedding."

Gasps filled the room as Violet turned toward Frederick Langley, who sat in the second row, his face a picture of confusion—feigned confusion, Violet noted. But there was a glint of something colder in his eyes.

"Frederick," Violet said, her voice cutting through the murmurs, "you planned the theft of the necklace to ruin Sophia's wedding. But this wasn't just about the necklace, was it? It was about revenge. You couldn't stand that she moved on, that she was marrying someone else."

. . .

FREDERICK STOOD, his expression darkening. "That's ridiculous," he said, his voice tight. "I had nothing to do with any of this."

Violet's synesthesia flared as she focused on him. The colors swirling around him were dark, deep hues of crimson and orange—deception and rage. But something else was there, too—fear.

"You USED the hidden tunnels to move the necklace and other stolen items," Violet continued. "You framed Alden because he saw you in the act. But you didn't plan for him to die, did you? That was an accident. He followed you, maybe confronted you, and you panicked. He got in the way, and you left him out in the cold to die."

FREDERICK'S JAW CLENCHED. "You don't know what you're talking about," he growled.

BUT VIOLET PRESSED ON, pulling out the final piece of evidence—the torn fabric from Sophia's gown. "This was found near the sculpture where Alden's body was discovered," she said, holding it up. "But it didn't come from Sophia's dress. It came from a garment that you had access to, something you used to get close enough without raising suspicion. You've been hiding in plain sight, using the staff and the tunnels to cover your tracks."

FREDERICK'S FACE twisted with anger, his mask of calm slipping away. "You think you can prove this?" he spat, his voice low and venomous.

Violet took a step forward, her eyes locked on his. "You've

already proven it yourself. Every time you tried to sabotage this wedding, every time you tried to hide your guilt, you left a trail. You didn't mean to kill Alden. He was just in the wrong place at the wrong time, wasn't he?"

FREDERICK'S HANDS curled into fists, but before he could respond, hotel security moved in, grabbing him by the arms. His struggle was brief, but the fury in his eyes told Violet that she had hit the mark.

As he was escorted out of the chapel, the air seemed to shift. The tension that had hung over the hotel for days began to lift, replaced by a stunned silence.

AFTER THE DUST settled and Frederick was taken away, Violet stood outside the Ice Chapel, the Arctic wind biting at her face. The case had taken more twists than she could have anticipated, but now, it was over. Sophia was safe, the necklace had been found, and the truth had been revealed.

BUT AS SHE reflected on the events, one thing lingered in her mind—the frozen body of Alden Graves. His death had been an accident, but it was no less tragic. Caught in the web of someone else's vengeance, he had become a casualty of a personal vendetta. The stolen necklace had been a smokescreen, but it had ultimately led Violet to the truth.

VIOLET GLANCED BACK at the hotel, its icy towers gleaming under the pale Arctic sky. She had solved the mystery, but the cold, both literal and figurative, still clung to her. The Ice Hotel, for all its beauty, had been a place of secrets and lies.

With a final breath, Violet turned and walked away, knowing there would always be more mysteries to uncover—ones that wouldn't always end with easy answers.

Frost & Found

Frost & FoundThe chill of the Arctic wind was beginning to lift, though the Ice Hotel still shimmered in the early morning light, its walls a testament to both the beauty and danger it had held within its frozen halls. As Violet Frost stood near the courtyard, watching as the hotel staff dismantled the last remnants of the crime scene, she couldn't help but reflect on how everything had unfolded.

The necklace, hidden inside an elaborate ice sculpture near the main ballroom, had been found just hours before. Its glittering diamonds catching the light through the carved ice had made it almost impossible to spot unless someone knew exactly where to look. Frederick Langley had been meticulous in his deception, hiding the necklace in plain sight while using the tunnels beneath the hotel to move undetected. His plan to ruin Sophia's wedding and frame Alden had been elaborate, but his motive—an old wound of rejected love and festering jealousy—was tragically simple.

. . .

Frederick had been taken into custody the night before, his protests silenced as the evidence mounted against him. The truth had come out, the pieces of the puzzle finally fitting together. And though the wedding continued, it had a different tone now—less jubilant, more introspective, as the guests whispered about how close they had come to being a part of something far worse than a missing necklace.

Violet walked through the courtyard, her breath visible in the crisp air, taking in the quiet now that the chaos had passed. The ice sculptures that had once felt like whimsical decorations now stood as silent witnesses to the dark secrets that had been hidden beneath them. The reindeer sculpture, where Alden's body had been found, had been carved away, the space now empty, as though to erase the memory of what had happened there.

As she reached the steps leading into the hotel, she paused, looking back at the grand structure. This place had tested her in ways she hadn't expected. From the biting cold that had gnawed at her bones to the maze of deception she had navigated, the Ice Hotel had been more than just a setting—it had been a challenge. One she had overcome.

Violet had always disliked the cold. It made her anxious, restless, and vulnerable. She had spent much of her life avoiding situations that pushed her too far out of her comfort zone, preferring to solve mysteries from the warmth of her small, cluttered office. But this case had forced her to confront not just the cold outside, but also the parts of herself she had been reluctant to acknowledge—the fear of failure, the uncertainty of navigating a world that often felt overwhelming with her synesthesia.

AND YET, here she was. She had faced the cold, both literally and figuratively. And while she was still bundled in layers of scarves and gloves, still not a fan of the freezing wind that whipped across her face, she felt a little less afraid of it now. Maybe the cold wasn't so bad. Maybe it had taught her something.

SHE TOOK A DEEP BREATH, her chest rising and falling with the sensation of crisp air filling her lungs.

INSIDE THE HOTEL, the wedding was finally taking place. Despite everything that had happened, Sophia had insisted on going through with the ceremony. The bride, now without her necklace but with a sense of relief that the chaos had ended, had managed a smile as she exchanged vows with her groom. It wasn't the lavish, carefree event she had planned, but it was real—tinged with the understanding that life could change in an instant.

AS VIOLET WATCHED through the grand ice windows, she saw the small group of guests gathered in the chapel, the soft glow of candlelight reflecting off the icy walls. The wedding was subdued, quieter, but there was still joy there, a reminder that even after all the darkness, people could move forward.

VIOLET SMILED TO HERSELF, turning away from the scene. She had done her job. The mystery had been solved, the thief caught, and the guests could return to their lives, albeit with stories they'd probably tell for years to come.

But for Violet, this case had been more than just solving a puzzle. It had been about finding herself in the midst of chaos. She had doubted herself at times, had felt the creeping chill of fear and uncertainty, but she had pushed through. Her synesthesia, once something that set her apart, had become her greatest tool. The colors, sounds, and sensations that flooded her senses had guided her, revealing the truth hidden beneath layers of deception.

And as she stood there, looking out over the Arctic landscape, she realized something else. She was capable—more capable than she had given herself credit for. The cold, the bizarre circumstances, the dangerous twists and turns of the investigation—she had faced it all and come out stronger on the other side.

Maybe she didn't love the cold, but she didn't hate it anymore either. The cold had forced her to confront her limits, and in doing so, she had discovered something warmer within herself—the confidence to take on whatever came next.

As she made her way back toward the main entrance, her phone buzzed in her pocket. She pulled it out and glanced at the screen—a message from her office assistant back home.

"Another case already. This one's warmer, though—a tropical island. Want to take it?"

. . .

Violet chuckled softly to herself. A tropical island sounded like the perfect escape after this Arctic adventure. But as she typed out her reply, she hesitated for a moment, glancing back at the shimmering Ice Hotel one last time.

Maybe the cold wasn't so bad after all.

With a small smile, she typed her response.

"I'll think about it."

As the sun dipped low over the Arctic horizon, casting the Ice Hotel in hues of pink and gold, Violet Frost walked away, ready for whatever mystery lay ahead. She had found the truth in the frost, and now, she was ready to face whatever warmth—or cold—the future had to offer.

Epilogue: Warmth in Unexpected Places

The Arctic sun hung low on the horizon, casting the Ice Hotel in a soft, golden glow that made it shimmer like a dream slowly fading. Violet Frost stood at the edge of the property, her boots sinking slightly into the snow, watching as the final traces of her time here seemed to melt into the quiet beauty of the landscape.

THE BITING cold was still there, but it didn't bother her as much anymore. She had spent days in this frigid world, navigating not only the physical ice but the emotional complexities hidden beneath the surface of people's hearts. She smiled softly to herself. The cold no longer felt like an enemy to be fought but something to coexist with, a backdrop to the more important, warmer things she had discovered.

VIOLET HADN'T EXPECTED to find warmth in a place like this. The Ice Hotel, with its towering, crystalline walls and labyrinth of frozen corridors, had seemed like the last place she'd find any sense of connection. Yet, the mystery she had unraveled here had brought out something in her she hadn't anticipated—a new layer of understanding, not just about the people involved, but about herself.

HER SYNESTHESIA, once a constant, chaotic flood of sensations, had been a gift during this case. It had allowed her to perceive the truth hidden behind deceitful smiles and charming facades. The swirling colors and sounds had guided her through each twist and turn, revealing the lies, the jealousy, and the motivations that had driven people to such extremes.

BUT MORE THAN THAT, this case had opened her eyes to the unexpected warmth found in human emotions—the vibrant hues of joy and sorrow, the intense reds of passion, the soft pinks of love, and the deep blues of regret. The world was a more colorful place than she had realized, and for once, the flood of sensations felt more like a comfort than an overwhelming wave.

THE COLD? Well, it still nipped at her fingers and made her nose tingle, but it no longer filled her with dread. She had found something within herself that was stronger than the Arctic winds, and that realization brought a small, satisfied smile to her lips.

AS SHE TURNED AWAY from the hotel, she heard the crunch of approaching footsteps behind her. It was one of the bellhops—a different one this time, one who had kindly carried her luggage when she'd first arrived. He handed her a small envelope, his breath fogging in the cold air as he nodded politely before turning back to his duties.

Violet frowned slightly, her fingers numb as she ripped open the envelope. Inside was a simple postcard, the image of a sun-drenched tropical island filling the front. Palm trees swayed gently in the breeze, the ocean a brilliant turquoise under the golden sun.

She flipped the card over.

"You're not done yet, Violet. Something warmer awaits you. See you soon. —A friend."

Violet blinked, surprised by the cryptic message. A friend? Her mind immediately went to the mysterious cases that always seemed to find her, like puzzles drawn to the only person capable of solving them. A warm island sounded like a world away from the frozen tundra she'd just survived, but somehow, she knew this was no ordinary vacation invitation.

Her heart quickened, excitement bubbling up. This was no coincidence—someone had already set the stage for her next adventure.

Violet tucked the postcard into her pocket, glancing one last time at the Ice Hotel, the place that had challenged her in ways she hadn't expected. As the sun began to dip lower, casting long shadows across the snow, she turned away, ready to leave the cold behind—but not the lessons it had taught her.

She felt more confident now, more capable of handling whatever mystery came her way, whether it was hidden beneath layers of snow and ice or buried in the tropical sands of some distant island. The warmth she sought wasn't just about temperature anymore; it was in the solving of puzzles, in understanding the complex layers of human emotion, and in the vibrant, colorful world of people's secrets.

As she walked toward the car waiting to take her to the airport, the chill in the air seemed a little less sharp, the cold less biting. She didn't mind it as much anymore. After all, she had found warmth in the unlikeliest of places.

With one mystery solved and another waiting on the horizon, Violet smiled to herself, her breath fogging in the Arctic air one last time.

Her next adventure was waiting.

The End.

Afterword: Reflections on Synesthesia

From the Desk of Violet Frost

Living with synesthesia has always been both a gift and a challenge, a vibrant, double-edged sword that cuts through my perception of the world in ways I never asked for but have come to accept. Imagine walking through life where every emotion, every lie, and every truth is not just felt but seen—colored, heard, even tasted. It's like living inside a painting where every brushstroke is someone's secret, every melody a flicker of hidden intent. Sometimes, the world is loud, too loud, and the flood of sensations can overwhelm. But other times, it's like a symphony, helping me unravel mysteries no one else could see.

THIS CASE at the Ice Hotel was a reminder of that. The cold, sharp blue of deception, the bright, jagged yellows of lies, and the deep reds of fear and anger—they were all around me. My synesthesia turned every interaction into a colorful map of emotions, guiding me, revealing things others might miss. It's what allows me to see past the surface, to understand people's true motivations even when they hide behind a smile.

But it's not all that easy.

Living with synesthesia is like living on a tightrope. In my personal life, the constant swirl of sensory input can make relationships difficult. Trust me, it's hard to focus on a conversation when someone's anxiety feels like blaring sirens or their sadness tastes bitter, like burnt coffee. I've learned to manage it, to let the colors fade into the background when I need to, but it never really stops. It's always there, making even the simplest interactions a little more complex. A little more colorful, sure—but also a little more exhausting.

Still, I wouldn't trade it. My synesthesia makes me a better detective. It helps me see the world in a way others can't, and in my line of work, that's everything. I've learned to embrace it, to use it as a tool, even when it complicates things.

The world is full of hidden truths, some painted in bright hues, others buried in the shadows. And with synesthesia, I get to see it all.

—Violet Frost

A Note from the Author

The character of Violet Frost came to life from a simple question: *What would it be like to solve mysteries if you could actually see emotions, hear lies, or taste fear?* I've always been fascinated by the idea of synesthesia—how the brain can mix senses, turning colors into sounds, feelings into tastes, and moments into sensory tapestries that are unique to each person who experiences them. For Violet, this blending of senses became the heart of her detective work. I wanted to create a character whose quirks weren't just charming but vital to how she solves mysteries.

WRITING a cozy mystery in such an extreme setting—the Ice Hotel, buried deep within the Arctic Circle—offered a fun contrast to Violet's colorful inner world. The stark coldness of the ice paired with the vivid sensory experiences she goes through allowed me to explore not just the mystery but also Violet's journey of self-acceptance. Despite her fear of the cold, she dives headfirst into the case, and in doing so, discovers new layers of strength she didn't know she had.

BLENDING synesthesia into the cozy mystery genre was a way to make every clue feel alive. Violet doesn't just notice a torn piece of fabric; she sees the emotions surrounding it. She doesn't just hear footsteps in the snow; she senses the tension in the air. It was important to me that her synesthesia was both an advantage and a challenge—a double-edged sword, much like how it is in real life for those who experience it.

I HOPE VIOLET'S JOURNEY—THROUGH the ice, through the mysteries, and through her own fears—resonates with readers. At its core, this story isn't just about solving a crime. It's about learning to embrace the unique parts of ourselves, even the ones we don't always understand. Whether it's synesthesia or something else, we all see the world a little differently. And that's what makes it interesting, isn't it?

THANK you for joining me in Violet's world. I can't wait for you to follow her on her next adventure—whether it's in the cold of the Arctic or somewhere a little warmer.

—EVANGELINE WINTERS

www.ingramcontent.com/pod-product-compliance
Lightning Source LLC
LaVergne TN
LVHW050026080526
838202LV00069B/6926